The Gathering Light at San Cataldo

Jeffrey Alfier

Blue Horse Press Redondo Beach, CA 2015

Also by Jeffrey Alfier

The Wolf Yearling,
Silver Birch Press, 2013

Idyll for a Vanishing River,
Glass Lyre Press, 2014

The Storm Petrel,
Grayson Books, 2014

The Red Stag at Carrbridge,
Kelsay Books, 2016

THE GATHERING LIGHT AT SAN CATALDO

JEFFREY ALFIER

Blue Horse Press
P.O. Box 7000 - 760
Redondo Beach,
California   90277

Copyright © 2015 by Jeffrey Alfier.
All rights reserved.
Printed in the United States of America.

Originally published by Kindred Spirit Press, 2012.
Reprinted by permission.

Cover art: "Ostuni Station in Winter"
by Jeffrey Alfier

ISBN   978-0692557259

For my Grandparents, Joseph and Anna Alfier

ACKNOWLEDGEMENTS

Grateful acknowledgment is made to the following journals, in which these poems originally appeared, or are forthcoming, sometimes in slightly different form:

Cairn   "Upon Your Return to Savelletri Harbor"
Cloudbank   "Last Arrival, Fasano Station"
dotdashdot (UK)   "Torre Canne, Once a Fishing Village"
Georgetown Review   "Winter in Sardinia"
Inclement (UK)   "Berthing the Skiff Named *Nonno Pasquale*"
Iodine Poetry Journal   "Early Train to Foligno;" "The Gathering Light at San Cataldo"
Penumbra   "Cathedral Beggar Outside Midnight Mass, San Pietro Bisceglie"
The Phoenix Review   "Letter from a *Pensione* to My Woman Back Home"

Cover photo: *Ostuni Station in Winter*, by the author. *Terraced Grove, Fasano, Italy*, and *Still Life for Itinerant* also by the author.

The author is grateful to Bloodaxe Books of Northumberland, UK, for permission to use the following copyrighted material: excerpt from the poem, 'Delos', from *Bernard Spencer, Complete Poetry, Translations & Selected Prose* (Bloodaxe Books, 2011).

The epigraph to 'Farmhouse in Lucania' is from "The Lithuanian Well," by Johannes Bobrowski, translated by Ruth and Mathew Mead, from *Shadowlands*, copyright © 1984 by Ruth and Mathew Mead. Reprinted by permission of New Directions Publishing Corp.

The epigraph to 'The Paving Stones' is from "Last Words from Maratea," by Richard Hugo, *Making Certain it Goes On*, copyright © 1984. Reprinted by permission of W.W. Norton & Company, Inc.

Special thanks to Tobi Alfier for tirelessly going over the manuscript and arranging the order of the poems.

CONTENTS

Upon Your Return to Savelletri Harbor / 1

Vagabondo / 2

Landscape with Lover at the End of Festa di San Nicola / 3

Twilight Beyond Mare Piccolo / 4

Torre Canne, Once a Fishing Village / 5

The Gathering Light at San Cataldo / 6

Calabria / 7

Winter in Sardinia / 8

Early Monday Train to Ancona Marittima / 9

Early Train to Foligno / 10

Watching From Via Monte Saraceno / 11

Late Diners at *Caffè Stella Cadente*, San Foca / 12

Cathedral Beggar Outside Midnight Mass, San Pietro Bisceglie / 13

Letter from a *Pensione* to My Woman Back Home / 14

Still Life for Itinerant (photo) / 15

Campomarino, Where the Sea Begins / 16

Apprenticed to the Sea / 17

Passeggiata / 18

Abandoned Farmhouse in Lucania / 19

To Fasano Through a Winter Field / 20

The Madonna in Apulia / 22

Torre Canne, Out of Season / 24

Pulling into Carovigno / 25

Berthing the Skiff Named *Nonno* Pasquale / 26

The Paving Stones / 27

Last Arrival, Fasano Station / 28

About the Author / 30

Terraced Grove, Fasano, Italy

And it was here by the breakers
That strangers asked for the truth.

Bernard Spencer, *Delos*

Upon Your Return to Savelletri Harbor

Make known to us the sea, *vecchio*.
How it summons you out past
the cobbled promenade,
its undulation through your dreams.

Tell us once again how cuttlefish
would darken the cracks in your mother's
plates, how flour wintered her knuckles,
her beauty the ragged scent of coming rain.

Cause us to glare at your bay
to see it warp the late light,
how it brims the silver-scaled wealth
of your nets.

From your night window, measure
the moon-splashed sea
as you tell your sons the virtue
of salt abrading your eyes.

Consider us, we pray, *vecchio*,
as your prow trolls beyond daydreams
of bluefin. Return, show us your hands,
let them give us their sea.

Vagabondo

On foot over broken coastal paths,
over cormorant tracks on shorelines,
comes the wanderer – *americano*,
overtaken at midday by hunger.

The rain-laced wind reels out
his lengths of sodden travel. Stony
roads of winter could weary him
into sleepwalking. Yet this sea-lit

dreamer still reaches for harbor
and sun, olive forests ascending
over clouds of wildflowers, time
free of unwinding clocks, or compass.

His woman, forbearing back home,
knows his return from the foreign
bounty that summons him to inscribe
what unfolds in the axis of his days.

This man, wanderer over stone,
will lie awake beside her and hear
wind glide through their window,
as if it needed something there.

Landscape with Lover at the End of Festa di San Nicola
Yes, I recall it was on Via Colonna

In the distance, fresh lightning
cleaved summer. Fellow pilgrims
of wine wavered through damp winds
that compelled them inside trattorias.

Dregs, in blood-red ferment, stormed
the bottom of homespun Corvina,
its grit like silt stirred by shark-panicked
fish. It settled coarsely on our tongues.

Above us, geraniums held out beneath
windows. Across the table, a deserted bowl
of grapes cupped rain that broke the surface
of wine. Our love never lowered its glass.

Twilight Beyond Mare Piccolo

The tired peasant walks his worn bike
homeward, perceives the warm surprise
of a ballad ascending a stone road that slopes
toward Taranto. Through the words,
he inhales the fish markets on Via Cariati

pressed into the humid smelter that is August.
They summon him to his youth again
before the future lost tolerance, this present
music the soft voice of what could never be,
glowing, lyrical, and his alone to sing.

Torre Canne, Once a Fishing Village

At night, boats moored along Via Del Mare
rock in the swelling surf like fitful dreamers.

Once more a fisherman drops in weariness
beside his wife. From their bedroom window

she watches lightning skein the Adriatic
as though in grievance with errant ships.

She knows her husband's hands were flawless
once, unburned by rope or salt, but redeemed

by the toil sleep secures him from. At first light
she'll release him to the sea, as dark as it is.

The Gathering Light at San Cataldo

Here is where blue glares, mists and breaks
into spindrift, red of Padre Pio and of rose
endures like footprints of an archangel.
Breakwaters shield a lighthouse, pilgrim
feet singe in penitence, and dust-mottled
sunlight washes through my mind
more unfailingly than thoughts of home.

At night, this peasant bread, this *Primitivo*
wine, seep my silent hours in the arid
sundown scents that circuit arterial streets
beyond my boardinghouse, their timeless,
ascetic stare from shuttered upper windows,
my shadow obscured, and my eyes hidden.

Calabria
    after Leonard Nathan

Near Brindisi, a young woman unseen
to me, sang faintly through the night
in the boardinghouse on Via Rondinella.
Taken unaware, I fell for her as rain
flooded nights in her dust-beleaguered town.

Unnumbered days after, in every trattoria,
I leaned into the dark eyes of women,
the rise and fall of their warm voices,
to see if she appeared among them
through all the laughter and smoke.

Signorina, your voice allied me to the gusty
coast beyond Calabria. Come nightfall
at some forgettable stop, I'll know again
the distance I've gained from your town,
and what was taken with so little music.

Winter in Sardinia
for Sandy

Storms sweeping Corsica don't spare us here.
Wind always triumphs if conquerors won't.
On this island, Catalan walls are drenched
just to sate silver-green supplications
of olive groves that swallow rivulets
threading moonlight on Via Sanzio,
that road we took home where rain lengthened steps
and heavy skies vowed torrents without end.

This town has girls too pretty to be real.
But your life is more luminous to me,
your hand my embrace where nothing is lost,
though earth wears-down our footprints in whispers.

Early Monday Train to Ancona Marittima

Dawn kindles clouds like breath over tinder.
A lark bursts from the stationmaster's roof
in the scarce currency of its pleated wings.

Workweek passengers amble to railcars
as though resigned to never return home,
minds tethered to clocks, numbered tracks.

My gaze drifts up to the lark, its wild flight
over a woman chasing the train, watching
me hold my breath with her eyes.

Early Train to Foligno

Roman dust, this easy flood of dawn, mean rail stations abide
with an acrid copper scent matched by brooding railcars,
their sides dented as if forever bearing the rage of cynical men,
each wheel at any speed protesting our movement,
in drawn-out wails, like mothers braying children home.

The rise and fall of pressure in our ears as trains cascade
through tunnels means Ancona junction can't be far off,
rain soaking our outdated map as we welter into afternoon
with switchmen remote in the easy distance, watching
us pass, and knowing their weather is never foreign.

Watching From Via Monte Saraceno
In Mattinata

How much darker the Adriatic becomes
fronting chalk cliffs that rise behind me,
almond and olive groves, and orchids

in dim luminescence as they stagger
through each other's shadows – satin
silhouettes cut by a full moon standing

silent over Castellucio. Far afield, it silvers
the seaside footprints of daytime children,
where tides resolve shorelines into grottoes,

the harbor town's roads ambling ever seaward,
waiting for the yield only dark waters whisper,
hope rising each day out of the morning light.

Late Diners at *Caffè Stella Cadente*, San Foca

Colored balloons ring the fence that circles
the terrazza where a woman feels a breeze
slip past her into the main dining room.
It cools those faithful to the convention
of supping late, an old world proverb of need
where waiters attend a couple who strain eyes
to read menus worn by years in other's hands.
They are man and wife – regulars forever.
The man slides his hand across the table
as he reaches, aware her touch will complete
the circuit. Outside, the woman on the terrazza
watches rising wind free a balloon. Adrift,
its silk-thin shadow brushes her folded hands,
the way unpinned hair falls over an eye.

Cathedral Beggar Outside Midnight Mass, San Pietro Bisceglie

It has always come down to this,
my linger in the cooling hours before
night stirs the faithful to shuffle past

my eyes that will watch them look away.
Streetlamp shadows lengthen toward
my palm where few coins will fall.

My walker beside me, not many notice
my foot, bent ninety degrees at birth,
as if poised to step into an unclaimed life.

I listen to hymns echoing behind me,
antiphons that blur in recital. Liturgy
escapes a sainted window above.

When Mass ends, the faithful quicken
their pace beyond my palm, the weight
of their silence like a prayer abandoned.

Letter from a *Pensione* to My Woman Back Home
Via Cenci, Fasano

A quick breeze in the deepening nightfall
glides through my unshut window, stirring
the handful of wild chicory and chestnuts
I'd gathered to smuggle home to you.

Leaning into night air, over the alley I watch
a woman's geraniums release petals in wind,
like the silk stockings she lets fall before
cupping her hand to light candle with candle.

Darling, I write to you on a napkin reddened
from the blood-rich spill of Calabrian
wine, press my palm against the pen's ink
to sleep with your name on my skin.

In a room two floors down, I hear a child
open her voice in a moonlit prayer. She too
leans into sundown, the end of her day
come to hands folded at an unlit window.

Still Life for an Itinerant

Campomarino, Where the Sea Begins

I could summon a final Fernet-Branca
before loosening my tie for a walk home
in the warm, moonshot night, my fedora tilted
back on my sweaty brow, luckier than the man
one stool over, his peasant pockets that buy
nothing but advice to go home, an empty glass
at arm's length, a demand not followed by supply,
his dark eyes that say, *this is all I've come for.*

Why must midnight clocks wear that deadpan
glare, the hard rhyme of hour and minute
against the day's unraveling hem, tomorrow
forecasting its own bitter cure, the bar's shelves
restocked before the city's old wake early to pray
the *Magnificat*, night birds over their streets
where a woman's glance is culled from shadow,
a loss of words that almost burns the tongue.

Apprenticed to the Sea

Angelo, you go home ghosting the scent
of your grandfather's nets and bluefin,

a scaling knife in your pocket, the blood
of unhooked gills stuck to your vest, hearty

breath of surf rhythmic behind your eyes.
You reach for the bottle of *Cinzano*

as you speak to the wildness of uncertain tides,
of kneeling in prows to plead the Virgin's help,

of being a mile offshore, a good day's catch,
the sudden drop into the trough of a wave.

Passeggiata

Not yet late into evening and already I've lost
my small sense of direction down streets
that skein a city growing populated

with walkers current-caught in foot traffic,
wading to piazzas from unseen doorways,
sunset's gray last light a dimming tributary

rising through windows above clustering
crowds, friends in delirious chatter that falls
un-translated into this stranger's ear,

the voices melding with thunder grumbling
down the distant Adriatic, threading the sharp
scents of fried zeppole, frittata and burning

olive branches where old men, hands wreathed
in blue veins clutch glasses of wine – red
from grapes rich with the blood-memory

of Vesuvius, turn their focus to a contadino's
son coming late into the streets, having waited
to watch his father rake fields into windrows,

my weak, broken grasp of their dialect hearing
of growing seasons, the next round of bocce,
how a widow always finds her candlelight.

Passeggiata – 'a light stroll', an early evening ritual in Italy where town folk emerge into the streets to meet with friends, often by chance, to share each other's world.

Abandoned Farmhouse in Lucania
> Quench me with earth.
>   Johannes Bobrowski

All that had been is now this,
buckling beams, the decay
of timber, rust of latch and hasp,
a tribe of sparrows that flush
from rafters like star-fall.

Out back, from thick shadows,
a chestnut tree drops its thorned
harvest for any taker on foot
or wing, the ripe fruit over tiles
where the last nails were driven.

To Fasano Through a Winter Field

February storm clouds wash
the sky into the ever-sundown
tints of a grayblue canvas.

The Italian hotel clerk told you
the quickest route into town,
but the street names fell foreign

from her tongue, annunciation
lost to you, streets that warp
to the gray torrent of stone

that conveys you through a wind
unsettling mandarin trees,
gusting a scarf's red plumage

across an old woman's face.
From a window, her narrowed
eyes tracked your first shortcut

through the gnarled majesty
of a timeless olive grove,
on past a farmer's dogs barking

from behind the flowerless
poison of winter oleander,
the ghost ship of their howls

coursing to a hidden moon.
On the balcony of the first
house you pass, bright yellow

seeps from a limoncello drink
left outside. A hunger inherited.
A dim light that steps away.

The Madonna in Apulia

I. Mater Dolorosa, Church of Our Lady of the Rosary

Flanking the nave, in your crestfallen
eyes we read the blood-memoried
night of Roman iron, plighted now
to your grieving supplicants. Your black
robe is seamed with the Seven Sorrows,
your heart impaled on a prophecy
that won't exhaust its fulfillment.
With night-clad arms collapsed
to your sides, the crown you wear
is more razor wire than radial axis
of stars. Prayers are wept at you,
adesso e nell'ora della nostra morte…,
intercession pled to your dark peninsula.

II. Queen of Heaven, Church of Saint Anthony the Abbot

From the sanctuary's elevated
alcove, your hand-carved
raiment is the soft unfettered blue
of the sky over risen Lazarus,
the luminous blue in the dim
gardens of the poor. Your flawless
opened hands are blossomed offers
of mercy, your head crowned with
a constellation of undying stars.
The faithful turn to adore you,
your anthem a poem sung standing,
the lines first chanted by angels.

III. Virgin of Revelation, Savelletri Harbor

In the hollow inlet, sculptured white,
you could've coalesced from spindrift
or ice, color's vacancy offset
by the single red flare of a votive
candle, your crown a wreath of tiny
light bulb stars. Your eyes are shuttered,
hands folded, attentive to the seafarer's
supplication. Prayers to you
are shouted through gales. They fall
about your shoulders that do not face
the sea. Perhaps for you, under
no cathedral less than sky, grief
is deadlocked between requiem
and shipwreck, the starlight behind
you almost burning into the sea.

Torre Canne, Out of Season

The horizon of the emerald ocean
is seamless with the silverblue flood
of sky's rumored storms, only wind

trawling the waters today to gust
shoreward beyond the stilled
beacon of the lighthouse. Spinning

weathervanes and the sweetness
of olive wood coals and chestnuts,
it gusts inland over the solitary

walker no one waved to when he left,
slowing around his neck, his eyes
glistening for an instant, in the rush of rain.

Pulling into Carovigno

He was shaken from sleep at daybreak
as the train lumbered to a halt, a soft-focus
dawn, Gypsy in a black fedora selling
windfall apples from a rotting crate.
There, he saw a woman in dark Carrera
shades step through the sun's dusty glare,
a familiar dress, an easy gait to her stride
as she entered a caffé east of the station.

He asked the Gypsy, musing far off
over his apples, if he'd seen her too –
his lover from southern Salento.
The Gypsy thought he was *bevuto*,
offered him the dregs of bad wine.

When the woman emerged, crossed
to a parking lot astride the station,
he saw that her eyes were all wrong,
the hair a bit too lengthy and a shade off,
and he thought himself overtired.

Then she slipped into a cab beside
an older man who kissed her hands.
He watched them disappear, heard
the conductor's voice ghost through
the train cars, heard wheels groan to life,
wondered if it was her he'd really seen,
why he'd crushed the flowers in his hands.

Berthing the Skiff Named *Nonno Pasquale*

He had long turned away from large
steel-hulled vessels that took him
too far out into naked, shoreless seas.

Now, settled shoreward, the late light
is fixed upon his skiff's oars folded
atop modest nets. His shadow

falls across the windy harbor cove.
White linens drying on a balcony
snap hard in a gaining breeze

that engages him homeward, friendly
voices hailing from doorways, windows;
his wife opening a blue front door.

The wind sweeps past her and on into
a bedroom where sea dreams fall nightly,
standing fast, like a vessel overdue.

The Paving Stones
> And you, straniero, why did you come?
> Richard Hugo

In faltering Italian that stumbled off
my tongue, I asked a contadina
the way to a street named Via Tobruk.
She said if I walked long enough my feet
would Braille their way from the stones,
so cracked and uneven it was as if each
had labored under a timeless dispute
with the ground in which it was set.

I discerned from kind eyes that she'd walk
me there. Diverting through side streets,
we braced against tightrope-narrow
doorways to let traffic pass. Scents
of roasted chestnuts and stracciatella
suffused alleys with a homesickness
that said the air could have been a kiss
I forsook too long ago.

When the street was found, I shook her hand
warm as hearthstones, smelled the wild
chicory and figs she'd picked that morning
near the sea, her story grown less remote
and foreign now. "Signorina, *come si dice*:
Do I still remain a stranger in your eyes?"
She said I could now find alone
any street I'd never been down.

Last Arrival, Fasano Station

I recall little of the train I took from Brindisi,
or the tired steps I made inside the station,
empty of all but the voice of an unseen
loudspeaker in a language I scarcely understood.
It may have asked me why I came here,
who I thought I'd find, or perhaps it simply
heralded the day's final train. Somewhere down
a corridor a door echoed shut, and halted train
cars made sounds of beasts gasping under burdens.
Outside, night bore the warm redolence
of fecund earth—forests of olive trees and market
crops. Perhaps it was mere want of sleep,
but in the distance I heard the Adriatic breathing
over the shoreline, over the lives of fishermen
that labored it. A world away from home, night
blossomed deep. Beyond the station parking lot
it seemed a dark wall guarded the sleep of farmers.
Entering the road that leads toward town, my hunger
already lodged inside the coming day, blood-red
wine at a café table where I looked into faces I trusted,
solely because they were unknown to me, bright
with mirth, and all the stillness sweeping out to sea.

About the Author

Jeffrey Alfier is 2014 winner of the Kithara Book Prize, judged by Dennis Maloney. He has been nominated for seven Pushcarts, and is a two-time nominee for the UK's Forward Prize for Poetry. In 2013, he was selected as a finalist for the Press 53 Poetry Contest. Publication credits include *Spoon River Poetry Review*, *Arkansas Review*, *Copper Nickel*, *Crab Orchard Review*, *december magazine*, *Emerson Review*, *Iron Horse Literary Review*, *Kestrel*, *Permafrost*, *Poetry Ireland Review*, *South Carolina Review*, *Southwestern American Literature* and *Texas Review*. He is author of *The Wolf Yearling, Idyll for a Vanishing River, The Storm Petrel -- Poems of Ireland*, and most recently, *The Color of Forgiveness,* co-authored with fellow editor Tobi Alfier. His latest work, *The Red Stag at Carrbridge -- Scotland Poems*, is forthcoming in 2016. He is an Air Force veteran of 27 years and a member of Iraq and Afghanistan Veterans of America. He has written training manuals as a government contractor, and once taught history for City Colleges of Chicago's European Division. He is founder and co-editor of Blue Horse Press and *San Pedro River Review*.

www.ingramcontent.com/pod-product-compliance
Lightning Source LLC
Chambersburg PA
CBHW061346040426
42444CB00011B/3122